# HELLO TREES

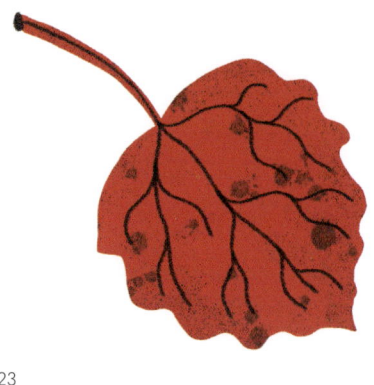

**LAURENCE KING**

LAURENCE KING
First published in Great Britain in 2023
by Laurence King

HB ISBN 978-1-51023-047-7
E-book ISBN 978-1-51023-080-4

10 9 8 7 6 5 4 3 2 1

Printed in China

MIX
Paper from
responsible sources
FSC® C104740
FSC www.fsc.org

Natural history consultants: Sarah Niemann and Derek Niemann

Laurence King
An imprint of
Hachette Children's Group
Part of Hodder and Stoughton
Carmelite House
50 Victoria Embankment
London EC4Y 0DZ

An Hachette UK Company
www.hachette.co.uk
www.hachettechildrens.co.uk
www.laurenceking.com

Nina Chakrabarti

# HELLO TREES

# A Little Guide to Nature

LAURENCE KING

# CONTENTS

*I think that I shall never see
a poem as lovely as a tree.*

**Joyce Kilmer**
(From the poem 'Trees')

# WHAT IS A TREE?

A tree is a plant with a woody trunk, branches and leaves.

LEAVES absorb sunlight and turn it into food for the tree.

ROOTS stretch far and wide in their search for nutrients and water.

The CROWN includes all the branches and leaves on the upper part of the tree.

BRANCHES hold the leaves, seeds, flowers and fruit of the tree.

The TRUNK is strong and supports the weight of the crown.

# AGE and HEIGHT

Given the chance, most trees live for a very long time. Some can grow to incredible heights.

**BRISTLECONE PINE**
*Pinus longaeva*

The bristlecone pine is found in the United States. It can live for up to 5,000 years!

In a forest, a tree has to grow taller than its neighbours to get more sunlight.

A mountain ash can grow to around 90 metres tall.

MOUNTAIN ASH
*Eucalyptus regnans*

you

# AMAZING SEEDS

As trees are not able to walk, they use other ways to scatter their seeds.

Some seeds fly with the wind beneath their wings...

They spin...

**ROSEWOOD**
*Tipuana tipu*

whirl...

...and twirl.

**FIELD MAPLE**
*Acer campestre*

**THE RESIN TREE**
*Dipterocarpus alatus*

**COCONUT**
*Cocos nucifera*

Others are heavy and roll down to the sea for a swim.

A lot of seeds come hidden inside the tree's tasty fruit. Animals eat the fruit, then poo the seeds out in a new location!

Some seeds are sticky or have hooks they use to hitch a ride on animals' fur.

Other trees grow their seeds in pods. The pods explode, spreading the seeds far and wide.

11

# SEED TO SAPLING

Seeds have a protective coat, which means they can stay dormant for months or even years.

They wait patiently for the perfect moment to pop out and grow.

A young tree is
called a sapling.

Behold, a tree is born! And unlike us humans,
it will continue to grow for the rest of its life.

# ROOTS

Roots anchor trees to the ground.
Without strong roots, trees would just fall over!

Most roots grow below
ground and spread
far beyond the
canopy of
the tree.

COMMON BEECH
*Fagus sylvatica*

## BANYAN
### Ficus benghalensis

The banyan tree sends long roots down from its branches to form new trunks. This means the tree can spread out over a huge area and makes it incredibly strong.

# SEED SPOTTING

Looking at seeds helps us identify
the tree that it came from.

**ELM**
*Ulmus*

**OAK**
*Quercus*

**CHESTNUT**
*Aesculus*

**LIME**
*Tilia*

**BEECH**
*Fagus*

**HOLLY**
*Ilex*

WATTLE
*Acacia*

MAPLE
*Acer*

PINE
*Pinus*

PLANE
*Platanus*

Next time you spot a seed on the ground,
see if you can tell who its parent is.

# LEAF SHAPES

SIMPLE LEAVES
have only
one blade.

BLADE

SMALL-LEAVED LIME
*Tilia cordata*

The large vein in the middle
of a leaf is called a MIDRIB.

LOBED LEAVES have divisions
in their blade but these
do not reach the midrib.

MAIDENHAIR
*Ginkgo biloba*

COMPOUND LEAVES are made up of multiple leaves or leaflets.

'Pinnately compound leaves' are feather-shaped.

**COMMON ASH**
*Fraxinus excelsior*

'Palmately compound leaves' are hand-shaped.

**HORSE CHESTNUT**
*Aesculus hippocastanum*

# LEAF PRINTS

**1.** Collect some leaves
of different shapes and sizes.

**2.** Put a layer of newspaper down
on your work surface to protect it.

**3.** Apply paint to one side
of the leaf using a small
paintbrush or a sponge.

**4.** Lay the painted side of the leaf on to a sheet of paper and place another piece of paper on top.

**5.** Press down firmly using your fingers or use a rolling pin.

**6.** Remove the top sheet of paper, gently pick the leaf up and admire the print below!

21

# WHY LEAVES CHANGE COLOUR

Take a walk in the woods in autumn and marvel at the amazing colours of leaves.

In SPRING and SUMMER, leaves produce a green pigment called chlorophyll. It turns sunlight into food for the tree.

WYCH ELM
*Ulmus glabra*

YELLOW BIRCH
*Betula alleghaniensis*

In AUTUMN there is less light, and trees stop making chlorophyll. As the green pigment starts to fade, other colours begin to appear.

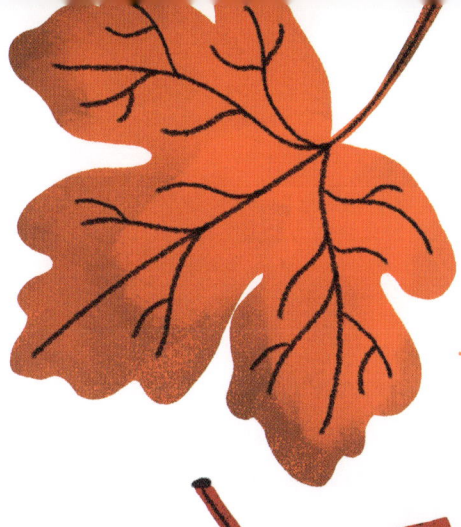

Carotene, which is also found in carrots, turns leaves ORANGE.

Anthocyanin turns leaves a marvellous RED.

As WINTER settles in, tannin makes leaves go BROWN.

When leaves turn brown, they die and fall off the tree. New leaves will grow next spring.

# DECIDUOUS and EVERGREEN TREES

Deciduous trees lose their leaves in winter,
but evergreen trees keep them all year round.

## ENGLISH OAK
### Quercus robur

The deciduous English oak in winter.

MONKEY PUZZLE
*Araucaria araucana*

The evergreen monkey puzzle tree,
native to Chile and Argentina.

# FLOWERING and FRUIT TREES

Some trees produce flowers that
grow into fruit we can eat.

**PLUM**
*Prunus domestica*

**CHERRY**
*Prunus avium*

APPLE
*Malus pumila*

PEAR
*Pyrus communis*

27

# FRUIT SEEDS

Inside every seed is a tree ready to grow.

PAPAYA

MELON

APPLE

MANGO

LEMON

POMEGRANATE

AVOCADO

PEACH

Next time you eat one of these fruits,
save the seeds and plant a tree!

# GROW A TREE

## METHOD 1 ✻ AVOCADO

**1.** After eating your avocado fruit, save the big stone (the pit) from the middle.

seed or pit

**2.** Give it a good clean and pierce it with four toothpicks.

**3.** Place the pit over a jar of water and change the water every two days.

**4.** After a few weeks, you may notice little roots growing. When the roots are bigger, move the pit to a pot with soil and watch your tree grow!

## METHOD 2 ✳ APPLE

seed or pip

**1.** Clean some apple pips and leave them to dry out for 1–2 weeks.

**2.** Fold the pips inside a moist paper towel and place in a sealable bag.

**3.** Pop the bag into the fridge for about a month. The pips like the cold!

**4.** Once the pips sprout, plant them in a pot with soil. When the seedling is big and strong, you can plant it into the ground outside.

31

# THE FOREST

Forests are found all over our planet and provide
a home for many animals, plants and fungi.

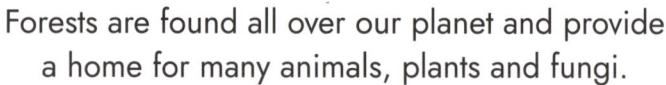

The UNDERSTORY is the layer
of trees under the canopy.
They receive dappled light
and grow at a slower rate.

The crowns of the tallest trees form a CANOPY and get the most sunlight.

The FOREST FLOOR is made up of small plants, ferns and mosses and hardly gets any sunlight.

33

# BARK RUBBINGS

Let's go to the park and make drawings with bark.

Take some sheets of paper and lots of brightly coloured crayons.

Place the paper over the tree trunk and rub a crayon over the paper.

Bark is like skin for trees! It's there to protect the tree against the elements.

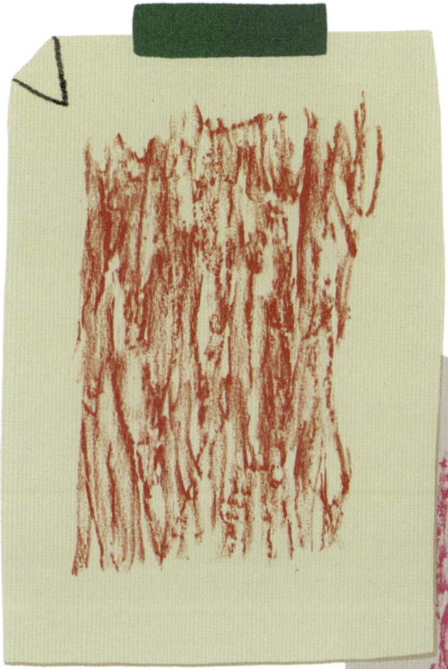

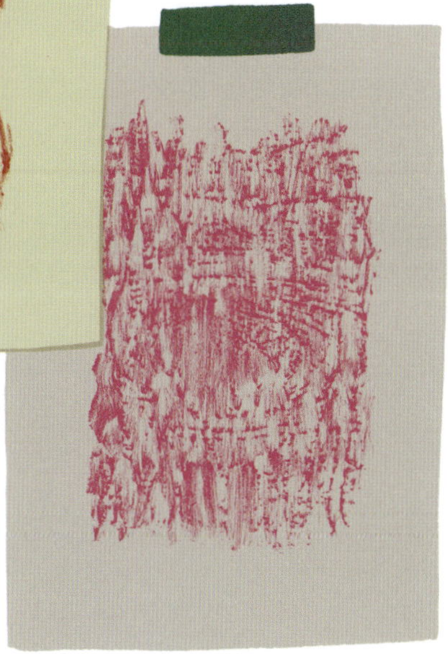

Look out for different kinds of bark — smooth, rough, scaly, bumpy and peeling are all good.

Have fun!

# CROWN SHYNESS

Some trees are careful not to touch the branches and leaves of their neighbours. This is called crown shyness.

Look up next time you walk in a forest or wood.
Can you spot any shy trees?

# SMELLY TREES

Trees release aromas to attract pollinators.
These ones smell particularly interesting!

smells like **rancid peanut butter**

smells like **dead fish**

**TREE OF HEAVEN**
*Ailanthus altissima*

**CALLERY PEAR**
*Pyrus calleryana*

WHITE SPRUCE
*Picea glauca*

smells like a skunk

smells of dog poo (female trees)

MAIDENHAIR
*Ginkgo biloba*

39

# SOME LIKE IT HOT

These trees love heat and sunshine.

The baobab tree stores water in its huge trunk to see it through the dry months.

AFRICAN BAOBAB
*Adansonia digitata*

Eucalyptus trees are native to Australia and are sometimes called 'gum' trees.

BLUE GUM
*Eucalyptus globulus*

## DATE PALM
*Phoenix dactylifera*

Date palms produce deliciously sweet fruit.

Olive trees are tough and can survive with very little water.

## OLIVE
*Olea europaea*

41

# SOME LIKE IT COOL

Conifers prefer chilly climates. They produce cones and have needle or scale-like leaves.

SITKA SPRUCE
*Picea sitchensis*

DOUGLAS FIR
*Pseudotsuga menziesii*

The magnificent trees you see here
are all conifers.

COAST REDWOOD
*Sequoia sempervirens*

GIANT SEQUOIA
*Sequoiadendron giganteum*

# CONES

When it is warm and dry, fir and pine cones open
up to release their seeds. When it is damp
or cold, the scales close up.

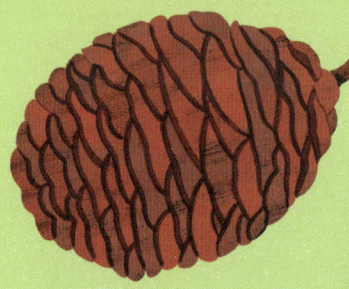

**CEDAR OF LEBANON**
*Cedrus libani*

**SITKA SPRUCE**
*Picea sitchensis*

**LAWSON CYPRESS**
*Chamaecyparis lawsoniana*

**BHUTAN PINE**
*Pinus wallichiana*

**DAWN REDWOOD**
*Metasequoia glyptostroboides*

**DOUGLAS FIR**
*Pseudotsuga menziesii*

**SCOTS PINE**
*Pinus sylvestris*

**SWISS PINE**
*Pinus cembra*

**GIANT SEQUOIA**
*Sequoiadendron giganteum*

**NORWAY SPRUCE**
*Picea abies*

**NOBLE FIR**
*Abies procera*

Next time you see some cones, pick up
a few and take them home to draw.

# TREES in FOLKLORE

In the past, people worshipped trees and believed them to be magical beings.

OAK

The king of the forest, the oak tree was considered sacred in many cultures.

ASH

The queen of the forest, the ash tree was believed to be a doorway into other worlds.

Elders would be planted in cemeteries to ward away evil spirits.

ELDER

46

## HAZEL

The hazel was believed to be a very wise tree, its nuts filled with magic.

Wands were made from yew wood and were used in ancient druid rituals.

## YEW

In ancient Celtic mythology, if you cut down an alder tree, your house would burn down.

## ALDER